Let us first acknowledge the Dja Dja Wurrung, the Traditional Owners of the Country where this story takes place. These people and their land were devastated during the gold rush.

Today the Dja Dja Wurrung are strong and their rangers still work to heal the damage from so long ago.

ABOUT THE ILLUSTRATIONS

So I could begin to imagine the Victorian gold rush through the eyes of Robbie, Jim, Charlie and Sam, I studied the finest goldfield artists of the mid-nineteenth century. The watercolours and prints of the incomparable S T Gill and the sketches and oil paintings of Eugene Von Guérard particularly inspired me. AW

ABOUT THE STORY

The characters and events in this story are as real as the nose on your face except for Ma Kilduff. I made her up. JK

To Susan Pepper – JK

To Don Gibb – AW

GOLD!

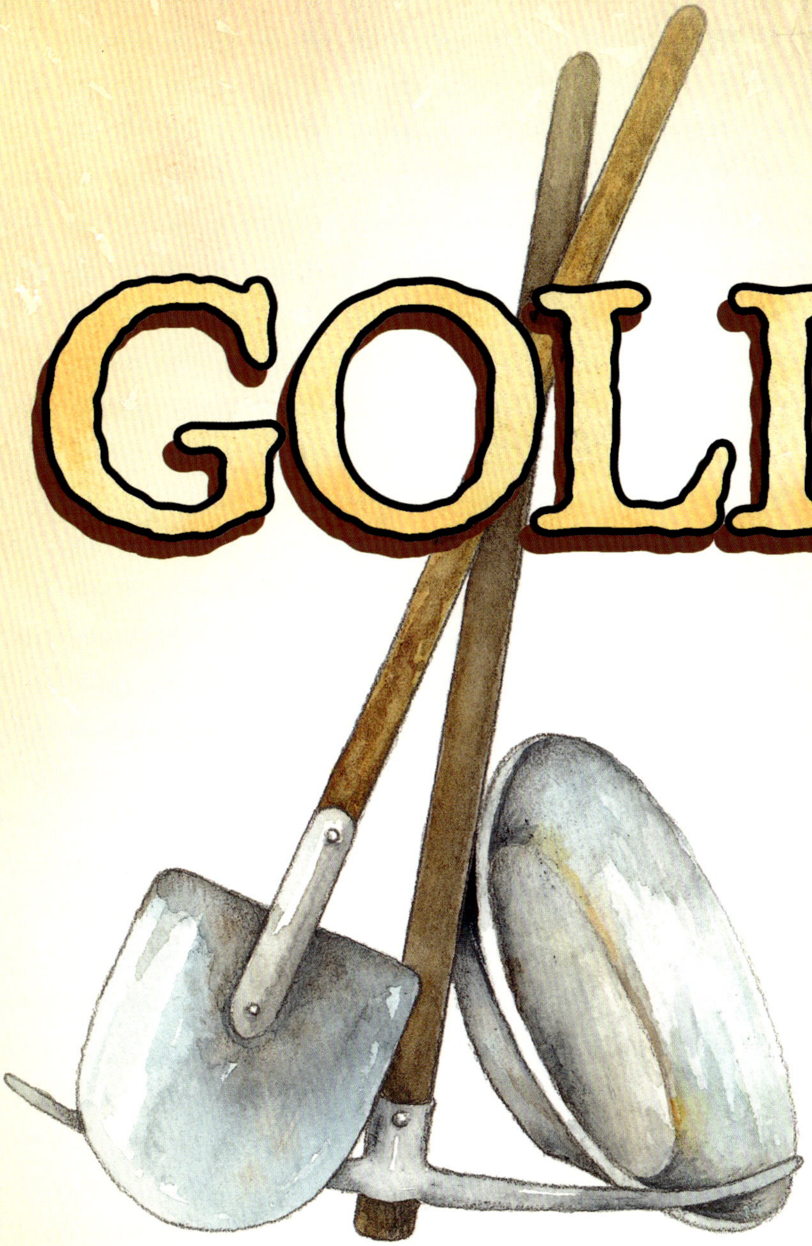

Jackie Kerin & Annie White

FORD ST

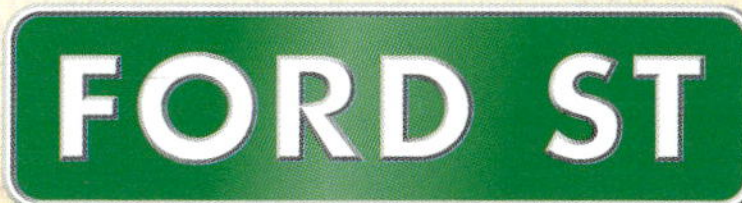

GOLD!

The wind snatches the cry from a creek bed and blows it to Melbourne town, then carries it across the seven seas.

GOLD!

The cry spreads to the north, south, east and west.

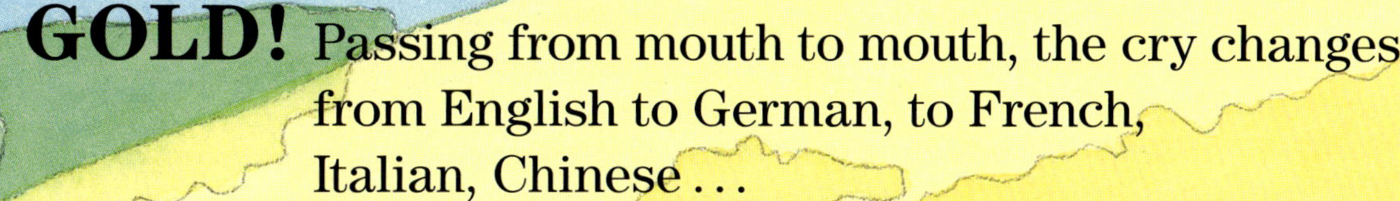

GOLD! Passing from mouth to mouth, the cry changes from English to German, to French, Italian, Chinese . . .

GOLD! In humble huts and grand palaces, the old and the young dream of riches and adventure.

'There's gold for the digging!'
'Nuggets like peanuts!'
'Plums!'
'Porcupines!'
'Ponies!'

Diggers arrive in their thousands.
Then with horse and cart, or bullock and dray,
or one foot in front of the other, the shepherds,
shopkeepers, postmen and professors,
plod to the goldfields.

'There's nuggets like bees!'
'Boots!'
'Baboons!'
'Buffaloes!'

Four young men, caught up in the rush,
meet on the road. Robbie and Jim Ambrose
have sailed all the way from England,
and Sam and Charlie Napier have
sailed all the way from Canada.

They pass over paddocks.
They pass through forests.
They pass by bare hills where eagles
circle in the wide, blue sky.

The brothers peel off at Buninyong, try their luck
at Ballarat, Barkers Creek and Bendigo.

And they find gold!

The size of a . . . fleck?
'Flea?'
'Freckle?'
'Fragment?'

'Is that another speck?'
'Pass the magnifying glass.'

Then a whisper reaches their ears:

'Kingower is the place to be.'

So on they plod.

'Our luck will change.'
'I smell it in the air.'
'I see it in the tea-leaves!'
'I feel it in my bones.'

When the four arrive at Kingower
they see toppled trees, piles of stones
and raw earth pitted with shafts.

'What'll we do?'
'We'll stake a claim.'
'We'll pitch the tent.'
'And tomorrow – we'll dig!'

They wake at dawn to the sound of warbling magpies.
Soon, Kingower echoes with the creak of winches,
the rattle of cradles and the swish of gravel in pans.

Men are whistling, women cursing,
children crying and thieves are watching,
sharp-eyed.

The brothers begin to dig.
It's January: the ground is baked hard,
and the work is backbreaking.

In February they moan:
'Could it get any hotter?'
'Could the flies be any thicker?'
'Could the smell be any fouler?'
'Could the thieves be any slyer?'

And just when they think
things can't get worse . . .
'Lads, it's parrot pie for dinner!'

Summer shifts to autumn.
They find a few small nuggets.

Ma Kilduff gives the young prospectors some advice.

'Don't hide yer gold under yer pillow. Thieves'll cut a hole in the tent and steal it while ye snore. I can promise ye that!'

June and July:
they wake to ice
in the billy can.
The diggers are
weary to the core.
Then one day
in August,
their luck
changes.

'Blimey!'
'Snakes alive!'
'It's big as a—'
'Shh! I've a plan.'

They fetch an old washtub and lower it down the shaft to Sam. He heaves the nugget into the tub and covers it with dirt. Jim, Robbie and Charlie take turns to winch up the tub, then they lug it to the barrow.

And in the bold light of day, they wheel the gold up to their tent.

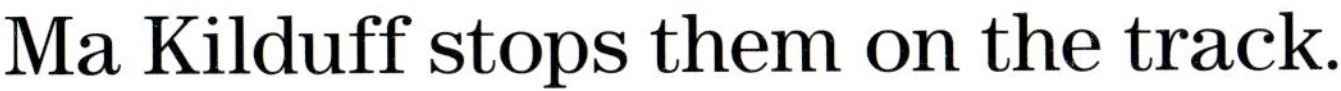

Ma Kilduff stops them on the track.

'Sew a pocket for yer gold
inside yer long johns.
Them thieves won't get it off ye there.
I can promise ye that!'
'That's a good idea, Ma.' The diggers look
down at their boots and up at the sky.
If she knew what they had in the barrow,
their secret would be out!

The brothers go to bed early
and pretend to sleep.
But at midnight,
they take out their shovels
and dig a deep hole inside the tent.
Quiet as dingoes, they bury the nugget.

The following morning they scratch their heads.
'What'll we do now?'
'Look for another.'
'For father and mother!'
'For sister and brother!'
'LET'S DIG!'

So the four lads dig.
They dig and dig and dig.

Deeper, deeper, deeper.

September.
October.
November . . . there is no more gold.

‘What’ll we do now?’
‘We’ll hire a horse and cart.’
‘We’ll take our gold to Melbourne.’
‘To the *bank*!’

They pass by bare hills where eagles
circle in the wide, blue sky.
They pass through forests.
They pass over paddocks.

When the bank manager
lays eyes on the gold,
he goes weak at the knees.

'It's bigger than a leg o' lamb!
Governor Barkly will
have to see this.'

Governor Barkly's heart skips a beat.
'It's the size of a . . . watch-a-ma-call-it!
My little girl Blanche will love this.'

Little girl Blanche claps her hands and says,
'Can we name it after me?
And can we show it to the Queen?'

The brothers agree.
'We'll call our nugget the
"Blanche Barkly".'
'We'll take it to England.'
'To show the Queen!'
'TO THE QUEEN!'

So Robbie and Jim, and Charlie
and Sam load the Blanche Barkly
aboard a clipper and set sail
for England.

In London, Queen Victoria invites the brothers to visit Buckingham Palace. 'What'll we do?'

Following a splendid meal, the Queen and her family gather around the Blanche Barkly. The Queen says, 'This nugget is as big as a badger! It shall go on show at the Crystal Palace for everyone to enjoy.'

The brothers can't believe how many people are queuing to admire their nugget.

Hurrah for the diggers bold,
We toiled through the heat and cold.
The people are milling
All clutching a shilling
To see our magnificent GOLD!

Meanwhile, back at the diggings,
Ma Kilduff keeps giving advice.
'Ye can put yer gold in a billy can
with a rotten fish and hang it up in a tree.
The thieves won't touch it.
I can promise ye that!'

The Dja Dja Wurrung: The Blanche Barkly was found on our land. Kingower is our word for the nearby hill. Thousands of gold diggers invaded our country. The creeks were turned to mud, the trees chopped down and our sacred sites destroyed. Many places in Victoria were renamed but many still have the old names.

Buninyong comes from the language of the neighbouring Wadawurrung and means *with their knees.*

Ballarat is also a Wadawurrung word and means *resting place,* or *reclining on the elbow.*

Sam: I found the nugget at 10 o'clock on 27 August 1857. The shaft was 17 feet deep, although some said it was only 13 feet. (That's between 4 and 5 metres.)

Charlie: Ours was the first really *big* nugget found in Australia! It weighed as much as a baby hippo and contained 1743 ounces of gold. (That's nearly 50 kilograms!)

In 1858 the 'Welcome' was dug up in Ballarat and contained 2200 ounces. In 1869 the 'Welcome Stranger' was found in Moliagul. It contained 2300 ounces of gold and is the biggest nugget ever found in the world.

Jim: We sold the Blanche Barkly in England for 12,000 pounds. It was on public display for a year but then it was smelted down and turned into 10,000 gold sovereigns. Today, that's over two million dollars' worth of gold. If you sold the sovereigns, they would be worth almost double that amount.

Blanche Barkly: My full name is Emily Blanche Barkly and I was seven years old when the big golden nugget was found.

Governor Barkly: When gold was found near Clunes in 1851, the government tried to keep it quiet. But word got out and the Victorian gold rush began.

People rushed off to every new goldfield to try their luck. Soon there weren't enough men left to sail ships or work farms or run businesses.

We made them buy a miner's licence for eight pounds for a year – that's a lot of money! – but it didn't stop them. There was a big fine if the police caught a miner without a licence.

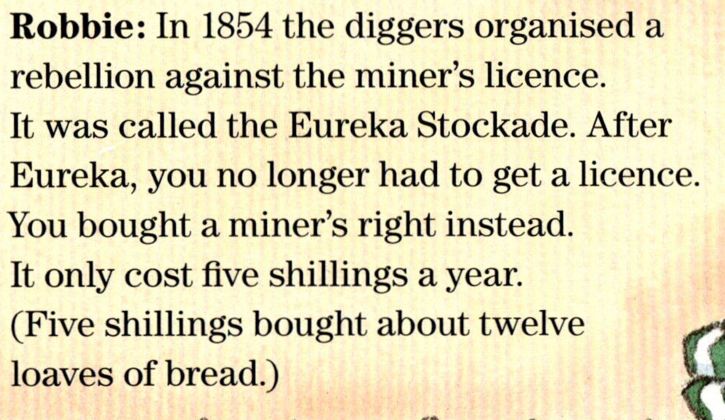

Robbie: In 1854 the diggers organised a rebellion against the miner's licence. It was called the Eureka Stockade. After Eureka, you no longer had to get a licence. You bought a miner's right instead. It only cost five shillings a year. (Five shillings bought about twelve loaves of bread.)

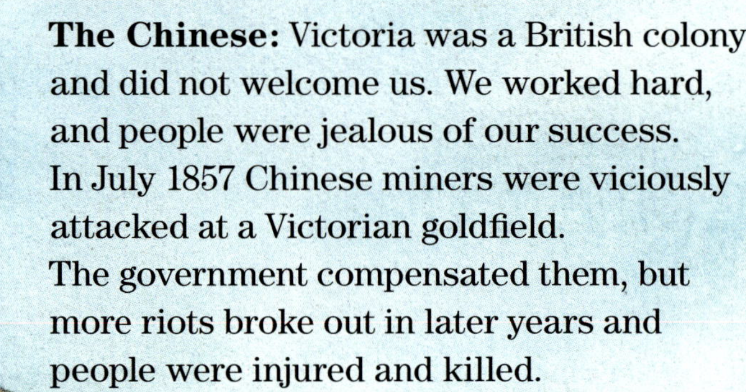

The Chinese: Victoria was a British colony and did not welcome us. We worked hard, and people were jealous of our success. In July 1857 Chinese miners were viciously attacked at a Victorian goldfield. The government compensated them, but more riots broke out in later years and people were injured and killed.

Prince Albert: The first Crystal Palace was built in 1851 in Hyde Park in Central London to house The Great Exhibition. I wished to impress the world and show them what Britain could make and build. After The Great Exhibition, the Crystal Palace was moved to Sydenham.

Queen Victoria: In 1854, I opened the
second Crystal Palace.
It was even bigger than the first.
Inside were displays about Ancient Egypt,
dinosaurs, circuses and cats – anything
you could imagine – from all over the world.
In 1858 the Blanche Barkly, one of the
treasures from Australia, was displayed.
(In 1936 the second Crystal Palace
was destroyed by fire.)
Ma Kilduff:
Keep yer eye out for the flickerin' candle.
It's the night fossicker. The thievin'
fellow sleeps all day and steals from
the best mines at night.

Ma Kilduff:
Look out for old mine
shafts in the bush.
Ye'll fall into 'em.
I can promise ye that!

First published by Ford Street Publishing,
Melbourne, Victoria, Australia

2 4 6 8 10 9 7 5 3 1

ISBN: 9781925804522 (hardcover)
ISBN: 9781925804539 (paperback)

Ford Street website: www.fordstreetpublishing.com
First published 2020

A catalogue record for this book is available from the National Library of Australia

Production design by Cathy Larsen Design
Printed in China by Tingleman Pty Ltd